Caithlin White

Illustrated by Ricky Audi

This book belongs to ....

This book is dedicated to all my fellow ADHDers
and neurodivergent friends, family and clients.

It's for those who went through school as the
"daydreamer", "disruptive", "fidgety and forgetful",
the "bad student" or essentially "just a bit different".

It is a celebration of you, of all your
strengths and fabulous quirks!

For more information visit: speechconnect.com.au

First published 2025 by Caithlin White

Copyright © Caithlin White 2025

All rights reserved. No part of this publication may be reproduced, distributed or transmitted in any forms of by any means, including photocopying, recording or other electronic or mechanical methods without the prior written permission of the owner, except in the case of brief quotations embodied in critical reviews and certain other non-commerical uses permitted by copyright law.

Produced by Independent Ink
Illustrated by Ricky Audi
Photography by Samuel Bryant
Typeset by Post Pre-press Group, Brisbane

White, Caithlin
My ADHD & Me/Caithlin White
ISBN: 978-1-7642186-1-0 (paperback)
ISBN: 978-1-7642186-0-3 (hardback)

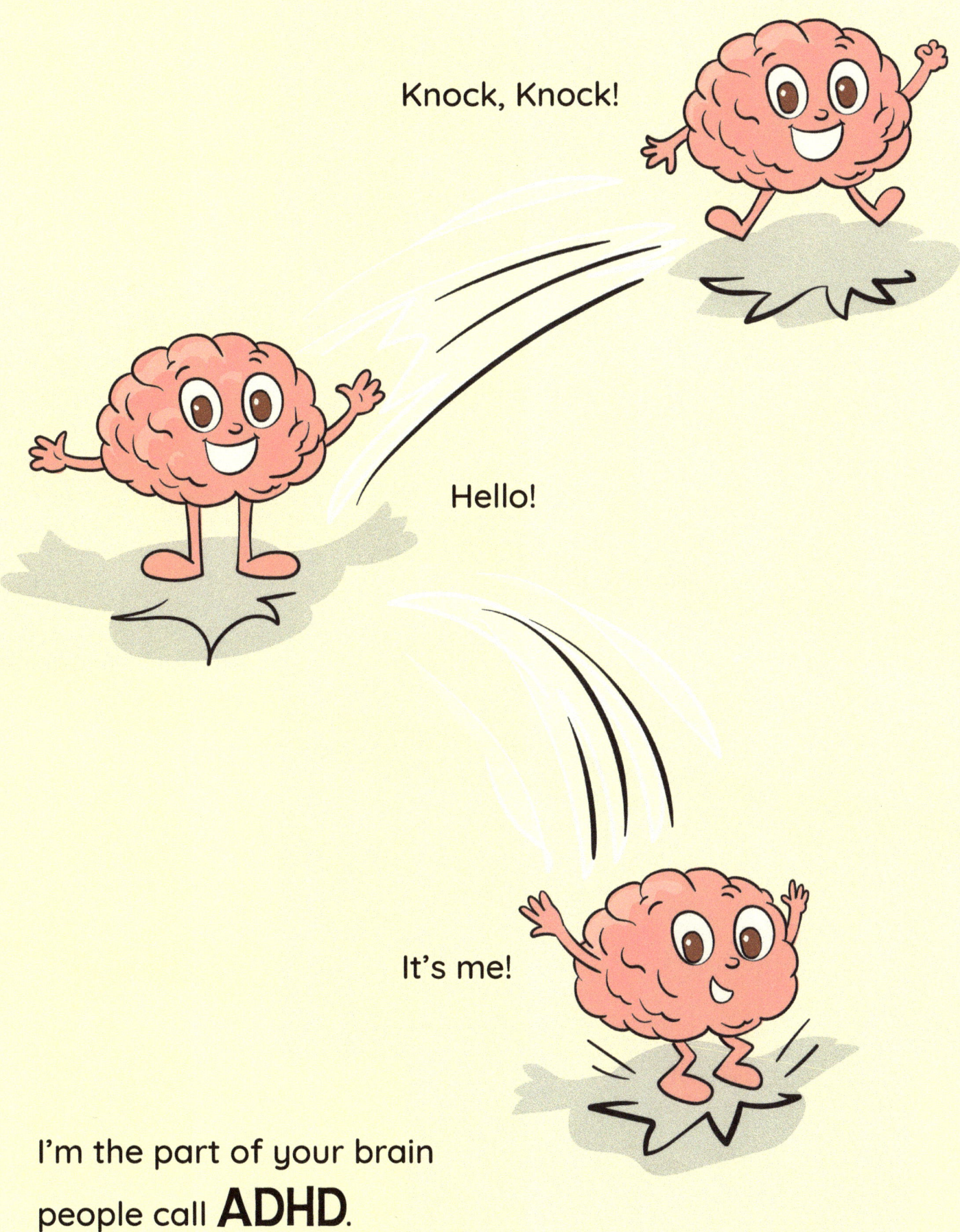

Knock, Knock!

Hello!

It's me!

I'm the part of your brain people call **ADHD**.

We are all different,
so we need to take time to see:

"What does it mean
to be exactly like me?"

It's great to have a brain like me,

For instance you can come up with amazing ideas ...

sometimes **INSTANTLY!**

And I help you engage with your hobbies
with passion and excitability.

With me you can explore the world of possibilities,

and you're good at making people laugh

when you do something silly!

Some things you may notice that relate to me are:

Hyperfocus,

Distractibility,

Impulsivity,

Interrupting,

Zoning out,

and fidgeting.

Having so many ideas can sure keep you busy,

and racing around can sometimes **leave you dizzy!**

With some things you may need patience from yourself,

(and sometimes others).

Some things you may find **tricky**:

getting out of bed in time to get ready,

forgetting things and leaving your room a bit messy,

becoming distracted
while someone is speaking,

or finding it **harder to concentrate** on something you're learning.

Because you want to grow up strong and healthy, it's important to look after your brain carefully.

So when your body is busy,
and you need some relief,

you can learn ways to feel calm,
and find a place of peace.

Some things that may help **your body feel at ease:**

eating something crunchy,

putting pressure on parts of your body,

taking a break to move your body,

lifting something heavy,

or holding something to **fidget** with.

You see, no one can see directly what's happening inside of you.

And some people think:

if you're **moving quickly,** or **zoning out,**

that you're not interested in what they're talking about.

Communication is Key

Other skills that help you to navigate the world responsibly,

are learning to communicate the things you need confidently.

It's good to tell people the important things,

explaining how you think can help avoid misunderstandings.

My brain is busy, but I love your stories!

When you talk to your Teacher,
you may want to say:

"I want to learn, but to focus
I need to do things a different way".

Other things you can say are:

Can I hold a **fidget** when I'm concentrating?

Can I have a **brain break** please?

Can you please write the steps so I can **see** them?

It's easier to focus when we **pause** the lesson for questions.

Some people I know may also feel calmer,

when they take medication with breakfast or after.

So if you're wondering if medication is right for you,

Talk with your Doctor

they'll know what to do.

Others supporting you may be:

OCCUPATIONAL THERAPIST

EDUCATION SUPPORT

SPEECH PATHOLOGIST

TEACHER

ART THERAPIST

So now you know a bit more about me.

Having a super brain like me definitely comes with fun and interesting things!

It also comes with a little extra responsibility.

I think if you can learn to see you brain as a key to being unique,

in the future, you will be capable of many amazing things.

So that's it from me

Have fun getting to know yourself on your journey,

And remember the very best people are those who ...

never ...

stop ...

learning!

About the Author

Caithlin is an ADHDer (with quite possibly other flavours of neurodiversity), but in the least, she is a neurodivergent Speech Pathologist. Outside of work Caithlin has ripped through different hobbies like it's going out of fashion. From learning French, Italian, German and Spanish, to dancing ballet, salsa, even playing the violin (very badly), and now acting. "An ADHD diagnosis made a lot of sense when I looked back at the range of interests I committed myself to so passionately. Realising this is also an ADHD trait made the diagnosis more beautiful too."

The great mystery of why she was so drawn to the space of working with Autistic and ADHDer clients was finally revealed a good 13 years into her career when she was formally diagnosed with ADHD in 2024. The final "aha" moment before the diagnosis, occurred when she was online with two ADHDer clients who began to dance together in skeleton costumes in a wonderfully unexpected and silly way. Realising how similar this creative, funny and quirky moment was to fond memories of her own childhood helped her see more positives that come with this neurotype. The click she felt with her clients over the years was then also obvious and so was her calling: *to support these unique souls to recognise their skills and to be fiercely proud of who they are.*

As she has been unmasking she is also adamantly supporting her clients to do the same. "When we spend time being who we are naturally and feeling accepted, and loved for this version of ourselves we can find great inner peace and confidence."

Note from the Author

Clinically, Caithlin has observed how often shame behaviours influence how her clients express themselves in the world. Shame can lead a person to mask who they are naturally which comes at a great cost to one's self-esteem. Masking is also extremely energy consuming. Sadly, too often, I see young clients masking and loosing connection with their authentic self. Questions like "will I ever be normal?" break my heart.

In relation to social skills and how we relate to others, someone must first feel confident in who they are before they can express themselves authentically. This is why I invest so heavily in supporting clients to identify qualities that make them who they are and help them to appreciate their unique traits.

Building skills that help us communicate more effectively with others is also essential for creating healthy friendships and social networks. How we socialise with others affects our self-worth, sense of value in the community and at large within society. Additionally, having poor social connections leads to isolation which contributes significantly to the mental health issues we see in the healthcare system.

Sure, we will all come into mismatch situations in life (and this has always been the case).

However, if someone can recognise their own communication style, I don't see why anyone should need to take a mismatch personally, or worse, internalise that they are "not good with people" or "something is wrong with them".

Having a unique brain can be a gift, and it can also feel lonely or isolating if others don't understand you, or what you need to feel calm and engage best within different environments. Bridging the gaps of misunderstandings and miscommunications in families, schools and other social environments children engage in is my passion. We are all made differently and if we can replace judgement with curiosity for the differences between each of us, I believe we can co-create a more open minded and accepting society in a greater sense.

My hope is that this book will support conversations within schools, family homes and even in therapy sessions around some of the unique ways in which we express ourselves and how we can all afford a little curiosity in situations where there is a break in joint understanding.

Yours,

Caithlin White

Terminologies Explained

Hyperfocus: Intense concentration and engagement within a task or activity. Hyperfocus is when your brain gets SO locked onto something interesting that you lose track of everything else around you – time, people talking to you, and other tasks.

In children, hyperfocus will often occur with technology use, particularly tablets, but could also occur with a strong interest such as drawing.

Distractibility: When your brain keeps getting pulled away from what you're supposed to be doing by other things – sounds, thoughts, movements, or anything that grabs your attention.

Technology particularly switching on the TV will often create a high level of distractibility for an ADHDer.

Impulsivity: When you act, or speak BEFORE you think – your brain skips the "stop and consider" step and goes straight to action.

You may notice impulsivity in children who reach out to touch computer screens or keyboards without considering consequences, other common examples include flicking game parts/counters.

Fidgeting: When your body makes small movements that you don't really control – like tapping, wiggling, or squirming – often without even realizing you're doing it.

Fidget toys are now very common, finding the right toy that provides input without distracting is the real challenge.

Zoning out: When your attention drifts away from what you are attempting to focus on. Zoning out may occur in conversation or may occur while reading. Often the person who zones-out will not realise this has happened until well after. If you can identify the types of conversations e.g. detailed topics you tend to zone out in, this can be helpful to share with people you regularly speak with.

Other Important Terminologies to Know

Masking: Refers to the process of someone, either consciously or subconsciously changing how they act, speak, and behave by replacing or concealing aspects of themselves. Masking is often used as a survival strategy to fit in or avoid perceived negative social consequences.

Neurotype: Refer to the type of brain you have e.g. Autistic, ADHDer or Neurotypical brain are each examples of neurotypes.

Neurodivergent: Neurodivergent brain types are those that are considered to be differently wired to the majority "neurotypical" brain type. The term is most commonly used to refer to Autistic or ADHDer types, however also encompasses other diagnosis such as Dyslexia, Dysgraphia, and mental health labels such as Obsessive Compulsive Disorder (OCD), mood disorders, and Post Traumatic Stress Disorder (PTSD), etc.

Did you know?

ADHD (Attention Deficit Hyperactive Disorder) is a neurotype that affects how the brain sustains attention, manages impulses and maintains the body's activity levels. It is one of the most common neurodivergent brain types in both children and adults. There are three subtypes of ADHD which can be summarised in the following groups:

Predominantly Inattentive

- Difficulty giving close attention to details, or frequently making careless mistakes
- Challenges remaining focussed in long activities, conversations or reading
- Often appears they aren't listening, even when spoken to directly
- Struggles to complete tasks such as schoolwork, or chores
- May be considered messy and/or disorganised
- Dislikes tasks that involve sustained mental effort: e.g. schoolwork, or completing forms
- Often loses things necessary for tasks e.g. pencils, glasses etc.
- Often distracted by external stimuli

Predominantly Hyperactive

- Frequent fidgeting or squirming in seat
- Often leaves their seat
- Often "on-the-go"
- Challenges engaging in play or leisure activities quietly
- Runs or climbs when inappropriate
- Excessive talking
- May answer before a question is complete
- Often interrupts or intrudes in conversations

Combination

A combination type presentation means the person's symptoms are evenly spread between inattentive and hyperactive, without having majority in either subtype.

References

Centers for Disease Control and Prevention. (2024). *Diagnosing ADHD*. Retrieved from https://www.cdc.gov/adhd/diagnosis/index.html

De la Peña, I. C., Pan, M. C., Thai, C. G., & Alisso, T. (2020). Attention-Deficit/Hyperactivity Disorder Predominantly Inattentive Subtype/Presentation: Research Progress and Translational Studies. *Brain Sciences, 10*(5), 292. https://doi.org/10.3390/brainsci10050292

French, B., Nalbant, G., et al. (2024). The impacts associated with having ADHD: an umbrella review. *Frontiers in Psychiatry*. https://www.frontiersin.org/journals/psychiatry/articles/10.3389/fpsyt.2024.1343314/full

Paul, M.L., et al. (2024). Incidence of Attention-Deficit/Hyperactivity Disorder Between 2016 and 2023: A Retrospective Cohort. *Psychiatric Research and Clinical Practice*. https://doi.org/10.1176/appi.prcp.20240121

www.ingramcontent.com/pod-product-compliance
Lightning Source LLC
Chambersburg PA
CBHW040000290426
43661CB00096B/1176